Fastest, Biggest, Lightest

~ The *Guinness World Records* Story ~

by Kirsten Anderson
illustrated by Gary Krejca

PEARSON
Scott Foresman

Editorial Offices: Glenview, Illinois • Parsippany, New Jersey • New York, New York
Sales Offices: Needham, Massachusetts • Duluth, Georgia • Glenview, Illinois
Coppell, Texas • Ontario, California • Mesa, Arizona

Every effort has been made to secure permission and provide appropriate credit for photographic material. The publisher deeply regrets any omission and pledges to correct errors called to its attention in subsequent editions.

Unless otherwise acknowledged, all photographs are the property of Scott Foresman, a division of Pearson Education.

Photo locators denoted as follows: Top (T), Center (C), Bottom (B), Left (L), Right (R), Background (Bkgd)

Illustrations by Gary Krejca

Photograph 21 Corbis

ISBN: 0-328-13372-8

Copyright © Pearson Education, Inc.

All Rights Reserved. Printed in the United States of America. This publication is protected by Copyright, and permission should be obtained from the publisher prior to any prohibited reproduction, storage in a retrieval system, or transmission in any form by any means, electronic, mechanical, photocopying, recording, or likewise. For information regarding permission(s), write to: Permissions Department, Scott Foresman, 1900 East Lake Avenue, Glenview, Illinois 60025.

6 7 8 9 10 V0G1 14 13 12 11 10 09 08 07

How large was the biggest spider ever found? What is the fastest-swimming fish in the world? How light was the world's lightest bird egg? How heavy was the world's heaviest bird egg? How many inches long was the largest corncob ever grown? And where in the world was the coldest temperature recorded?

The book *Guinness World Records* contains the answers to these questions. Published each year, this book is a **compendium** of **trivia.** Trivia are fun and amusing facts. A compendium gives a lot of information in a small amount of space.

The trivia found in the *Guinness World Records* compendium are the kind that are superlative. Things that are **superlative** are the most, or *-est,* of anything. So the book contains trivia about the larg*est,* small*est,* short*est,* and tall*est* of anything and everything in the world.

What about the huge spider that we first asked about? According to the book, the biggest spider ever was found in 1965. It measured eleven inches across. That's the size of a large frying pan!

And what about the world's fastest fish? The book says that the cosmopolitan sailfish has been measured at speeds of 68 miles per hour. A fish that fast can keep up with a car on a highway!

Keep reading to find the answers to the rest of the questions on page 3, as well as many other interesting facts about *Guinness World Records.*

 What about the lightest bird egg ever? A canary egg weighed 0.0009 ounces. And the heaviest bird egg ever? An ostrich egg tipped the scales at five pounds, two ounces. That means the heaviest bird egg was almost *six thousand* times heavier than the lightest!

Are you curious to know how many inches long that corncob was? *Guinness World Records* says it was 36.25 inches. That's more than three feet!

Finally, just how cold was the coldest temperature ever? The book says it hit -128 degrees Fahrenheit in Antarctica in July 1983. That's 188 degrees below Earth's average temperature of 60 degrees Fahrenheit!

We've answered all of the questions from page 3, but there's another question that needs to be asked. The question is: How and when was the first *Guinness World Records* put together?

The year was 1951. Sir Hugh Beaver was visiting some friends, and they argued about a question. The question was: Which bird can fly faster, the golden plover or the grouse? Some said the grouse was faster, and others said the golden plover was faster, but no one knew for sure!

Sir Hugh tried to find out. He searched libraries for the answer, but not one of the books that he read was of any help.

Sir Hugh was amazed that not a single book had the answer! He thought more about what had happened, and he thought of how much people liked to argue over trivia.

It was then that Sir Hugh had his great idea. He thought it would be wonderful if someone would write a book that listed answers to trivia questions!

Sir Hugh worked for the Arthur Guinness Company, and he told the company about his idea. The company liked Sir Hugh's idea so much that it agreed to pay to have the book written and published.

Sir Hugh then told his idea to Norris and Ross McWhirter, twin brothers who were British writers and fact-checkers. Sir Hugh asked the McWhirters to write the book, and the McWhirters agreed!

The first *Guinness World Records* was published in August 1955, and it became a bestseller within a few months! The book has been published every year since then. More than 100 million copies of the book have sold in 100 countries, and the book has been **translated,** or rewritten, into thirty-seven different languages.

What kinds of things make it into each year's book? The book is divided into categories, such as nature, science, and buildings. There are records about money and movies, there are pages about amazing humans and pets, and there are also many sports records listed.

What you won't find in *Guinness World Records* are records that required people to risk their lives. The people who write the book do not want people to risk their lives, and they will not write about records that involve endangering human life.

We've now answered the question of *what* makes it into the book, but there's still the question of *how* records get into the book. Also, how do readers know that the records listed are true?

There are two types of records listed in *Guinness World Records.* One type is simple facts, and simple facts are easy to check.

For example, the book lists India's Meghalaya state as the rainiest place on Earth. Meghalaya averages thirty-nine feet of rain each year, which is more than an inch of rain every day!

The average yearly rainfall in Meghalaya is something that scientists have measured. It is a simple fact that has been proven through observation.

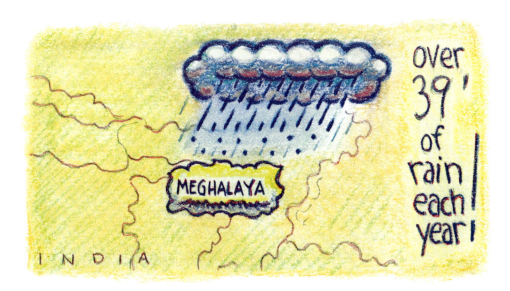

Another simple fact involves the heaviest hailstone ever. A piece of hail weighing over two pounds fell in Bangladesh in 1986. People weighed it, and then someone reported the hailstone's size to *Guinness World Records.* Once *Guinness World Records* verified, or made certain of, the hailstone's size, the record was put in the book.

But what if, after another hailstorm, other people find a hailstone that weighs more? If they can prove to *Guinness World Records* that the hailstone weighs more, then their hailstone will set the new record for the heaviest hailstone.

Many records listed in *Guinness World Records* involve people who have performed a stunt or a trick.

The record for the largest number of tap dancers dancing at once was set in Germany in 1998. It was set by a group of almost *seven thousand* tap dancers dancing together!

The book contains many records of that kind. At any time, any of these records could be broken.

For example, in 1997 a man in Sri Lanka stood on one foot for almost seventy-seven straight hours. But there could be someone out there who has just finished standing on one foot for seventy-eight straight hours!

The second kind of record found in *Guinness World Records* is less simple. This kind of record lacks exact information.

For example, it is listed that families in Egypt have kept Saluki dogs as pets for over five thousand years. But we will never be able to find the first family that did this. Therefore, we will never know the exact year a Saluki first became a family pet.

For the record to be broken, scientists would need evidence that Salukis were kept as pets before the people of ancient Egypt kept them as pets.

To show how much easier it is to verify some records than others, consider the record of the largest dog ears ever measured.

Mr. Jeffries, a basset hound, had his ears measured in 2002. Each ear measured over eleven inches from base to tip. That's the current record, but if there were a dog with larger ears, a ruler could be used to prove it.

You might wonder whose records are put into the book, or you might even wonder if *your* record could be in *Guinness World Records.* The good news is that anyone's record can be in the book! All you have to do is follow the proper procedure. A **procedure** is the steps you take to do something.

First, think of a record that you think you can break or set. It may be a record that you've already read about and want to break, or you may have a totally new idea for a record to set. Once you decide what record you want to break or set, ask your parents for permission to write to the people at *Guinness World Records.*

You will need to use the official form found on the *Guinness World Records* Web site (www.guinnessworldrecords.com). The form is also included in *Guinness World Records*.

The form asks you to describe your idea. It is important that you use as many details as possible in your description. That way it's easier for *Guinness World Records* to understand what you have in mind.

For example, you might want to build the world's biggest snowman. You should explain on the form how big your snowman will be and when and where you will build it.

When *Guinness World Records* receives your form, people there will review it. It is important to be patient while waiting for their reply. You may not have an answer for about two months. That's because *Guinness World Records* receives about sixty thousand forms every year!

When *Guinness World Records* writes back to you, you will know if your idea has been accepted. If it has been accepted, your record, if set, may be in *Guinness World Records!*

How can you improve the chances that *Guinness World Records* will like your idea?

First, make sure to suggest something that is not dangerous. As you have read, no one at *Guinness World Records* wants anyone to get hurt while attempting to set a record.

Guinness World Records also needs to be able to prove your record. Your idea must be something that can be counted, measured, or photographed. You must show that you did what you say you did.

Finally, your idea should be something that people will be interested in reading about. Remember, people all over the world read *Guinness World Records*!

The people at *Guinness World Records* are very interested in records that can be broken. It's exciting when someone attempts to break an **existing** record. An existing record is one that is still standing, or in place. People like stories of records that are challenged.

When someone breaks a record, it is a great accomplishment! An **accomplishment** is something special that you or someone else has done. Even if someone fails to break a record, it's OK because the failure makes the record seem even more special!

No matter what, you shouldn't feel disappointed if your idea is not accepted. Each year's book contains over four thousand records—so many, in fact, that there isn't enough space to list them all every year. A record may be printed in the book one year and left out the next year.

Also, you can write to *Guinness World Records* as many times as you like. You may have many different ideas, and other than the postage stamp, it doesn't cost anything to send in an idea. Who knows? One of your ideas may lead to a record printed in *Guinness World Records!*

Kenny G played the longest note in music history (45 minutes and 47 seconds) on his saxophone.

Now Try This

Set Your Record!

Are you ready to set a personal record? A personal record is set by doing the best that you can do in any one activity. Your personal record may even be a step toward a bigger record—maybe a world record! Here's how to set your personal record.

Choose an activity. It could be something from a sport, such as the number of successful free throws made in a row playing basketball.

You may set a goal to be accomplished over a long period of time. For example, you might read as many books as you can within a month or a year. There are many things you can try!

Here's How to Do It!

Make a journal to keep track of your effort to set your record. Label a page in your journal *Personal Record One.* Divide the page into three columns.

In column one, list the steps you plan to take to set the record. You could include the amount of time you will practice or work at setting your record. You could write about the steps you will take to meet or exceed each day's goal.

In column two, write the final goal you wish to reach. Explain all of the requirements you'll need to meet in order to set your record.

Work as hard as you can to set your record! When you reach your goal, write the date you set your personal record in column three.

Then you can start all over again and set a different personal record!

Glossary

accomplishment *n.* something special that someone has done.

compendium *n.* something that gives a lot of information in a small amount of space.

existing *adj.* being currently alive, present, or in place.

procedure *n.* a way of doing something.

superlative *adj.* the best or most extreme of something.

translated *v.* changed or rewritten from one language to another.

trivia *n.* fun and amusing facts.

verified *v.* proved that something is true.